SOUL ORIENTED SOLUTIONS

A Handbook of Quick Formulas to Use in Times of Emotional Crisis

RHEANNI LIGHTWATER

SOUL
RESOURCES

Albuquerque, NM
www.SoulResources.org
www.IntuitiveLearningCircle.com

The formulas set forth in this book should not be considered as an exclusive method of treatment. The appropriate medical or psychotherapeutic authorities should be consulted for the diagnosis and treatment of any medical or psychological condition.

The information and practices described in this book are best considered as an adjunct to orthodox medical or psychological treatments.

ISBN 978-0-9777080-7-9

ATTENTION ORGANIZATIONS, CHURCHES, UNIVERSITIES AND COLLEGES: This handbook is available as a download from:
www.SoulResources.net
or
 www.IntuitiveLearningCircle.com

Additional Titles Available:

Soul Prayer Charts
Gifts from the Rainforest
Keys to Prosperity Consciousness
Magic Circles Telling Stories
Intuitive Learning Games

Contents

Preface ~ 5

Intuitive Learning Circles and Graphs ~ 7

Formula #1: Coping with Serious Illness or Loss ~ 9

Formula #2: Stabilizing after a Traumatic Event ~ 17

Formula #3: Clearing an Overwhelmed Mind ~ 32

Shock ~ 43

Panic Attacks ~ 45

In Conclusion ~ 47

Preface

The purpose of this handbook and the Intuitive Learning Circles and Graphs is to tap into the innate healing capabilities of human beings. In both my professional and personal life, I have found that this ability, beyond anything else, has the potential to make or break the success of any endeavor.

When I first began this area of study in 1998, I already had eight years of experience as a Somatic Educator, working with people whose bodies had suffered from traumatic experiences - everything from emotional and physical abuse, to sexual abuse and post-traumatic stress. I learned how the body forms patterns of contraction and hyper-extension to compensate and protect itself from pain. I found out that the memory of a traumatic event is held in the tissue and perpetuated through stress messages that are routinely sent through the central nervous system like a continuous feedback loop.

It became apparent to me as I worked that our impulses and immediate reactions to situations are based upon past experiences. In a traumatized person, the body is like a puppet being led around on strings until the stress message can somehow be intercepted and resolved.

Likewise, there are bits of important memories that become frozen through shock, leaving the body in a state of amnesia, where it literally forgets how to work properly. This explains numerous structural and functional imbalances that limit range of motion, strength and the ability to follow through with a particular movement. More importantly, I noticed that people with this kind of physical amnesia are also predisposed to giving up very easily when it comes to their goals and hopes for the future. It's as if the mind has also forgotten how to be vital and follow through.

I observed recurring episodes where physical and mental symptoms would erupt, seemingly without warning. However, upon deeper investigation, the episodes were almost always triggered by an event or person that brought back memories of a past traumatic event. It seemed that the mind and body were definitely working together on some unknown level to sabotage any efforts made towards full recovery.

At the time, I was working through my own learning disabilities resulting from early life trauma. I had suffered from dyslexia for as long as I could remember. My mind would often go blank and anxiety attacks were frequent and debilitating.

One day, I decided that no matter what, I would find a way to bridge the gap between the limited life I was living and the life I dreamed of having. I decided that I would search every avenue that might bring me into contact with that unknown level where mind and body meet and rectify the damage that had been done. At the time, the books all said that victims of trauma and abuse could never fully recover, that they would at best, just learn to live with it. But, I wasn't willing to settle for that answer.

I pursued every modality available to me, including Hypnotherapy, Cranial-sacral Therapy, Structural Integration and dozens of other forms of bodywork. I learned about Homeopathy and put myself in the care of a fine Homeopathic Nurse Practitioner in Los Angeles.

Anything that held promise, I investigated tirelessly. Eventually, I came into contact with various forms of indigenous healing - Hawaiian, Peruvian, Chinese, Tibetan and Japanese - just to name a few. I meditated, learned kinesiology, and began writing about what was working and why. I studied dreams and symbology, shamanism and theories about the collective unconscious. Each modality was helpful in their own way, yet I kept having trouble holding ground. I would do all right for a while, but then I'd fall back into the same old patterns.

What was needed was a quick, easy way to focus my attention and retrain my mind to function in a healthy, balanced manner.

The Intuitive Learning Circles and Graphs

Soul Oriented Solutions is a booklet of three formulas that retrain the mind and help people to process emotional trauma by using the Intuitive Learning Circles and Graphs. Briefly, the method works by gently interrupting negative brain activity and replacing it with positive input.

The circles and graphs provide a positive framework for refocusing attention and recovering mental balance. Going through a sequence or formula calms the emotional centers of the brain, which significantly reduces stress and allows one to think more clearly.

The formulas can be used in certain situations to manage long-term feelings of hopelessness. The three situations that are covered are:

~ Formula #1: Coping with serious illness or loss.

~ Formula #2: Stabilizing after experiencing a traumatic event.

~ Formula #3: Clearing an overwhelmed mind.

As a bonus, two extra Circles are included that give short term relief for shock and panic attacks. When used in combination, the circles and graphs can help to alleviate post-traumatic stress and its accompanying symptoms including:

· Feeling fear about the future
· Over-dependence on drugs or alcohol
· Insomnia or nightmares
· Feelings of guilt or helplessness
· Uncontrollable crying
· Flashbacks
· Shock and feeling overwhelmed.

The therapeutic action that occurs while going through the formulas allows the viewer to slow down, sort out their thoughts and gain some insight about what they need to do for themselves next.

It isn't necessary for a counselor to be present, although doing so can be very beneficial since the formulas are easily integrated into most current crisis intervention methods. Additionally, the formulas provide a loose structure for sharing concerns and making positive plans for the future. Those who choose to use Soul Oriented Solutions on their own are encouraged to keep a journal to mark their progress and keep track of the good ideas that often come to mind.

Here is how the technique works.

The geometric pattern of the circles and graphs bypass your critical mind and bring relaxation to your autonomic nervous system - the part that is responsible for controlling bodily functions without conscious direction, such as breathing or your heartbeat. Once you relax, the image acts like a map where your conscious and unconscious mind can meet and come into balance with each other. Then, the accompanying question or affirmation stimulates your cerebral cortex, igniting possible solutions and allowing your critical mind to release negative thoughts and feelings.

The images work by having you breathe deeply while looking at each one in sequence for one to two minutes. Each one is accompanied by a simple phrase or question that supports and encourages you to calm down and think clearly again.

We have tested these tools extensively in clinical and classroom settings, with both children and adults. In many cases, they have been the extra step that helped to transform chaotic, destructive situations into ones of greater health and harmony.

Patients who were ill and preparing for surgery have successfully used these formulas to help them understand how to take better care of themselves and keep a more optimistic attitude. Some of the formulas have been utilized like navigational tools, providing preparation and acceptance for difficult life changes such as moving, death, divorce, or job loss. They have also been helpful for individuals recovering from childhood sexual abuse by helping them to manage the symptoms of PTSD.

Keep in mind that each person has a different response when using the circles and graphs.

Many people report that they move, rotate, vibrate or even change colors. This simply means that they are working and stimulating brain activity. Just keep gazing at the image until it appears normal to you. You might want to journal or discuss the thoughts and ideas that come up with a friend or counselor. However, make sure you finish the formula. Each one has a beginning, middle and end, so it's important to complete the entire sequence.

It is common for anyone working with the Intuitive Learning Circles and Graphs to experience an outpouring of pent up emotions, tiredness or even a physical release. Some people experience nothing during the process and respond later on, so make sure you allow plenty of time to rest. Drink plenty of water and get some exercise.

If you are a counselor, facilitator or volunteer, you might want to use the formulas to help your clients. If you do, be sure to go through Soul Oriented Solutions yourself first. That way, you'll have an understanding of what the experience might be like for them and will better anticipate any questions they may have about the process.

You may find that they help you as well. It's very common for significant insights to occur. Notice your thoughts as you look at each image. You might get ideas that could be very useful to you, your organization, or your clients.

Formula # 1: Coping with Serious Illness or Loss

Use this formula when you are:
  ~ Managing symptoms from a long-term illness
  ~ Preparing for surgery
  ~ Coming to terms with a significant loss or death.

Directions:
  These circles and graphs are here to help you whenever you are feeling anxious, upset or overwhelmed. Look at each one in the order given for one or two minutes. While you're looking, breathe deeply.

  The images may move, rotate, vibrate or change color. Don't worry. That happens sometimes. It just means that they are working to help you feel better. You don't need to do anything else right now.

  If you want to calm down and think more clearly, start with Formula #1 and then go through Formula #2 and 3. When you're done, you may feel much better. You might also feel tired or sad. That's okay too. It means that you're feeling safe enough to rest.

  Some people have gotten a lot of extra support out of going through this entire formula every day for twenty-one days. It helps to retrain your mind to think more positively and keep you on track toward your full recovery.

1. Breathe deeply, all the way to your belly while you look at this circle and then exhale.
Do that several times and relax.

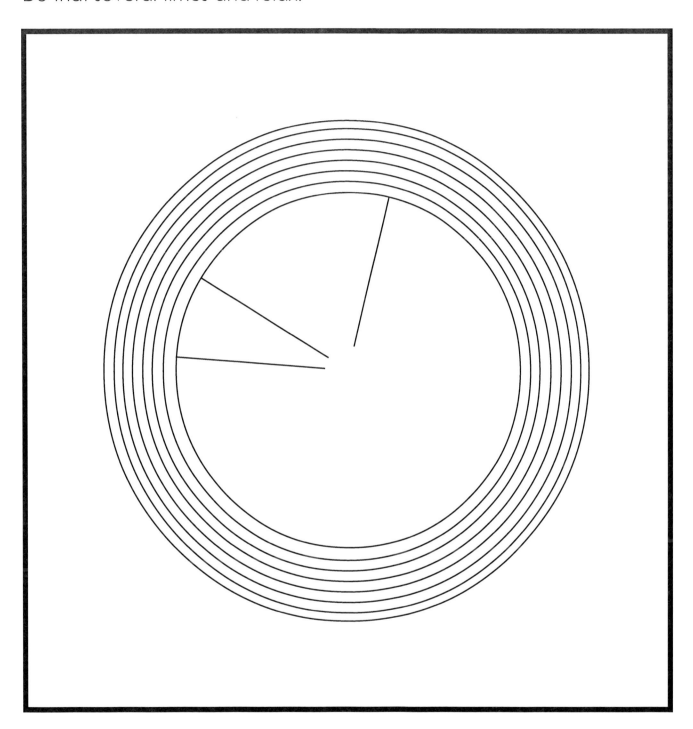

Asking for Help

2. Imagine that you can bring healing into all parts of your body, mind and spirit while you continue to breathe.

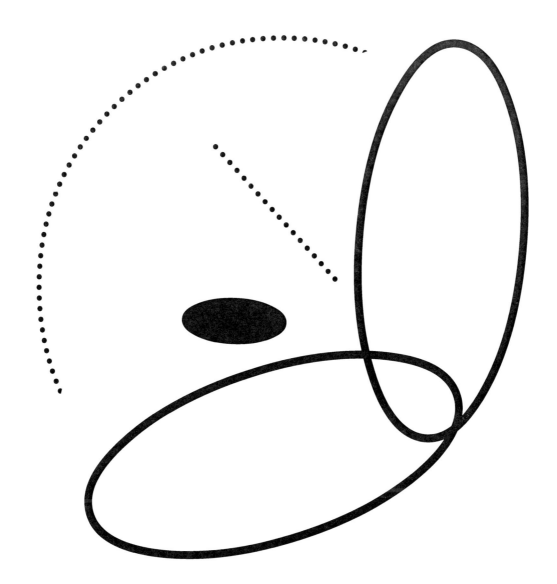

Support

3. Make a list of all your burdens.
Let go of anything that is bothering you right now.

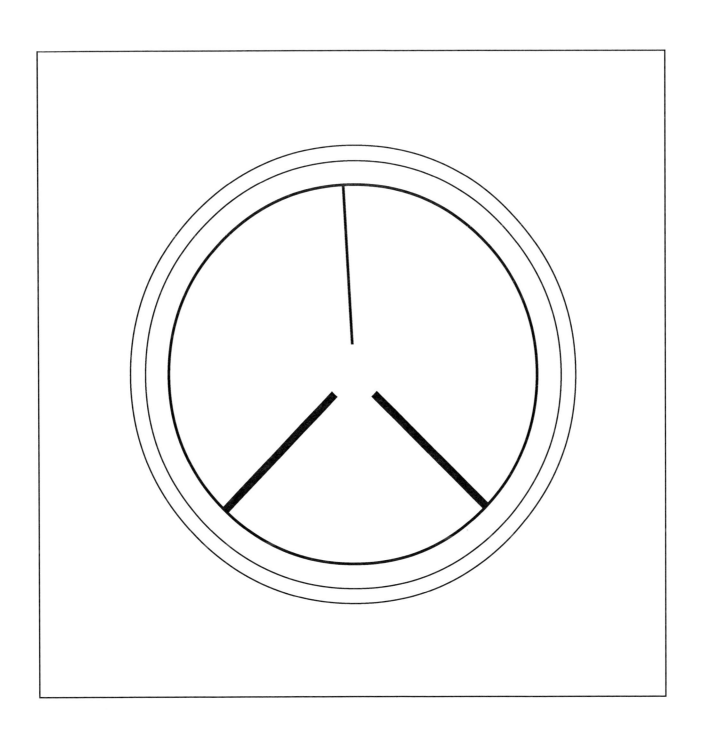

Peace

4. Breathe again.
Feel a calmness coming over you.
You feel calmer and calmer with every breath.

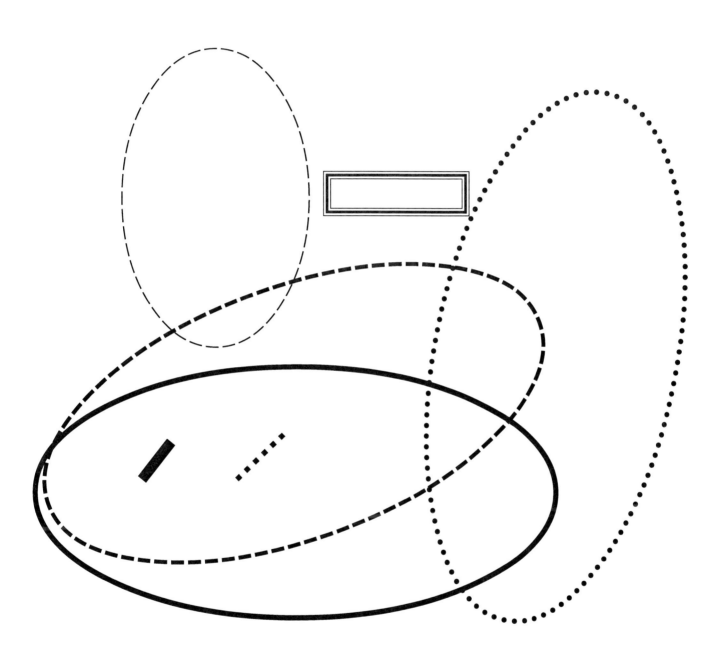

Balance

5. Visualize yourself as healthy and whole.

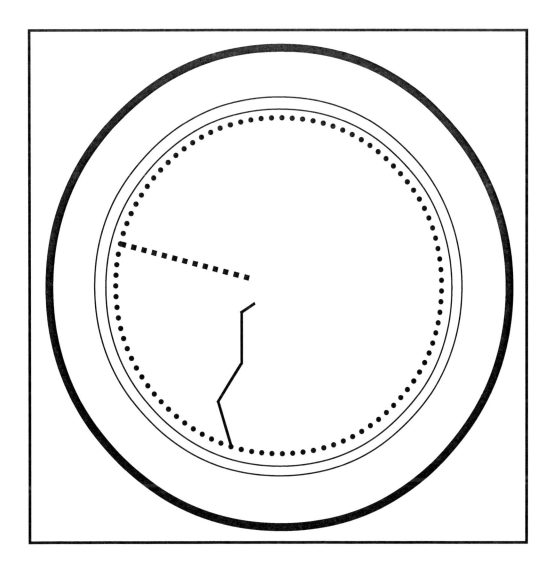

Hope

6. Send away any illness or pain that you are experiencing.

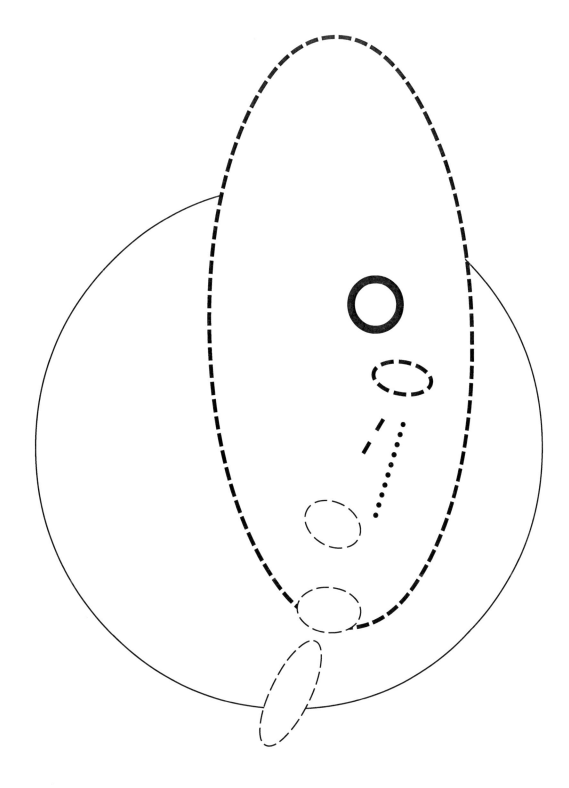

Cleansing

15

7. Fill yourself with strength and the knowledge that you are loved.
Let yourself rest now.

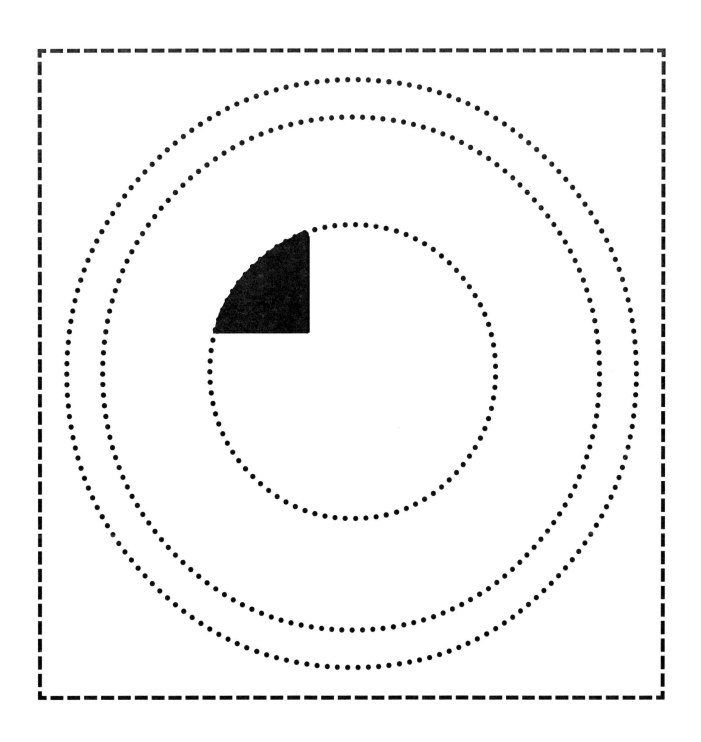

Faith

Formula # 2   Stabilizing After a Traumatic Event

Use this formula when you are:
- ~ Feeling lost or hopeless
- ~ Out of balance
- ~ Anxious
- ~ Upset
- ~ Weakened and want to regain your strength.

Directions:

Go through this formula with some paper and something to write with. Look at each image and notice any thoughts or feelings you might have in response to the words that accompany it. Be sure to write them down.

You might want to use this formula like a prayer or request for help. Remember that help doesn't always come the way you expect it.

1. Begin by taking a few deep breaths.
Gradually feel your strength returning to you.
Stronger and stronger with each and every breath.

Strength

2. Notice where you are right now. How old are you?
Feel your hands open and close.
Notice the time.
Bring yourself into the present.

Presence

3. What do you need right now?
What would help you the most?

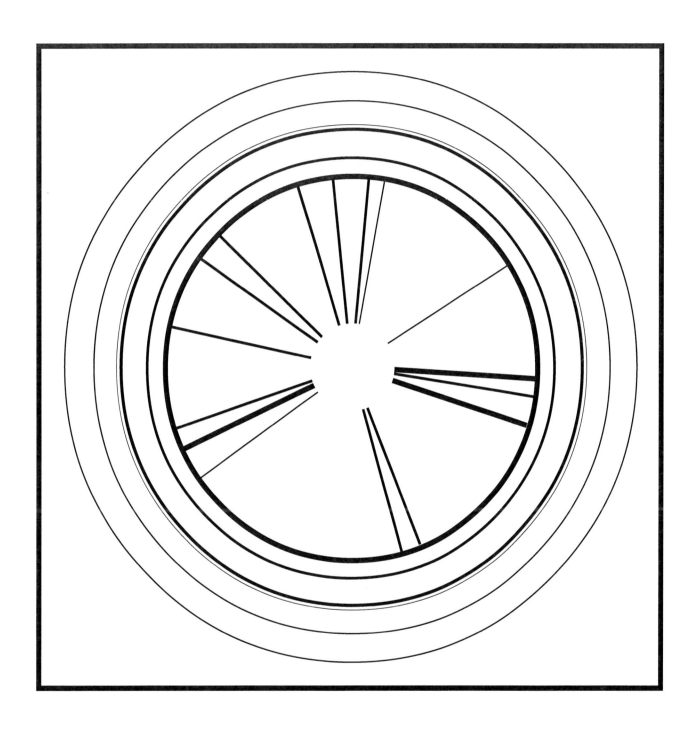

Courage

4. Do you know what has happened to you?

Recognition

5. How are you feeling?
What would help you to feel better?

Faith

6. Describe how you would like to feel.
Let yourself imagine what that would be like.

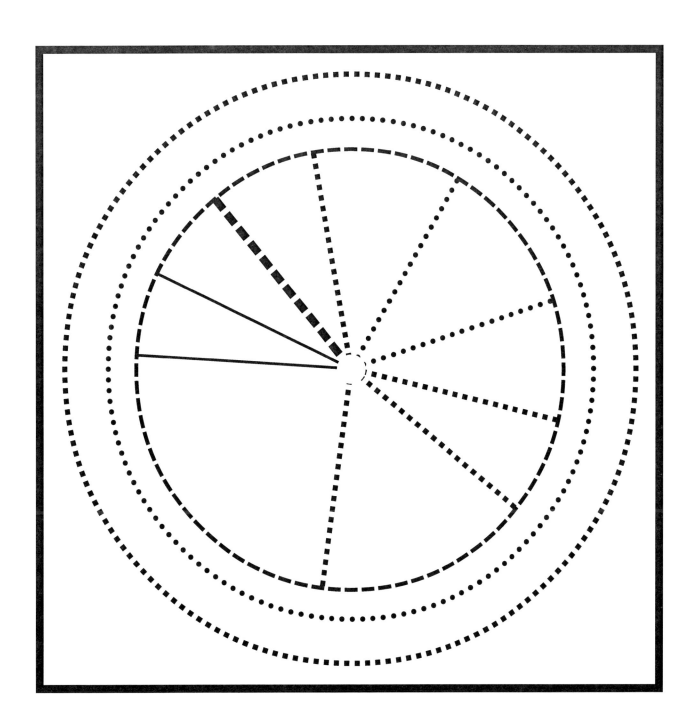

Focus

7. What do you want to have happen?

Clarity

24

8. Is there anything else that you want to ask for?

Communication

Nourishment

10. Focus all your energy on taking good care of yourself.

Strength

11. What will help you to take good care of yourself?

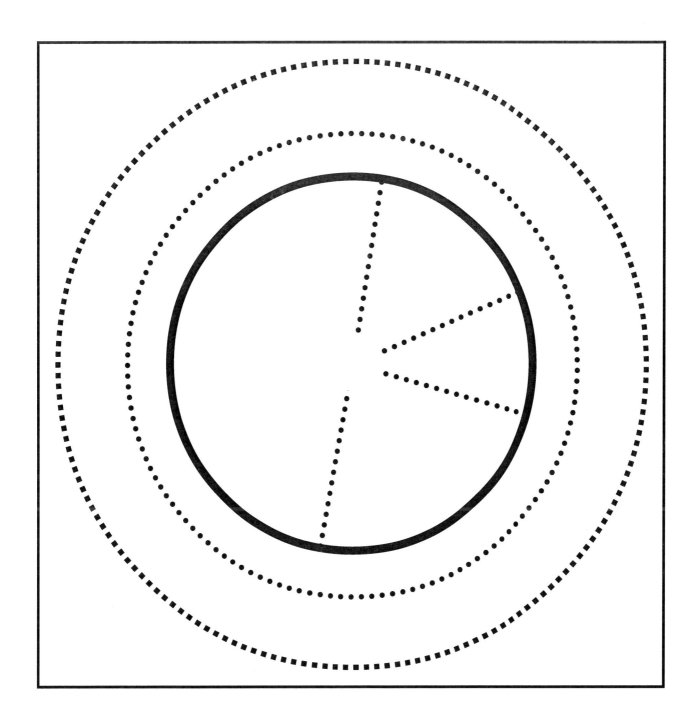

Receiving

12. What is stopping you?

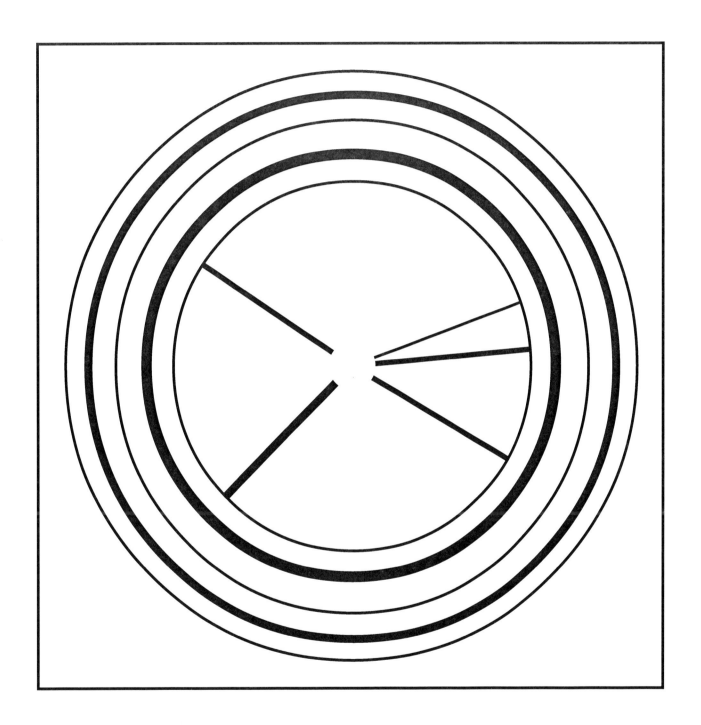

Courage

13. Make a list of everything you need.
Keep looking at the circle until you run out of things to write down.

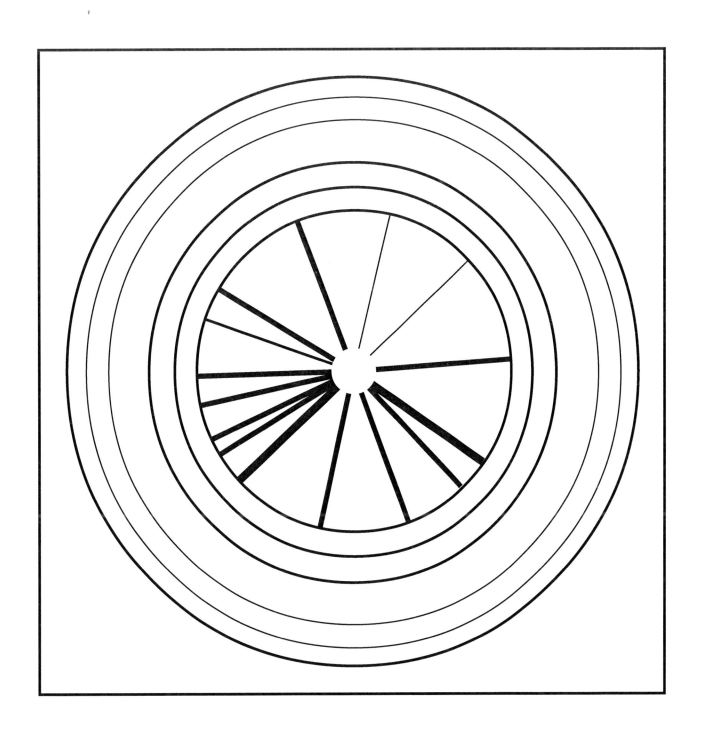

Assistance

14. Let peace and hope be with you.
Let them fill your heart with strength and courage.

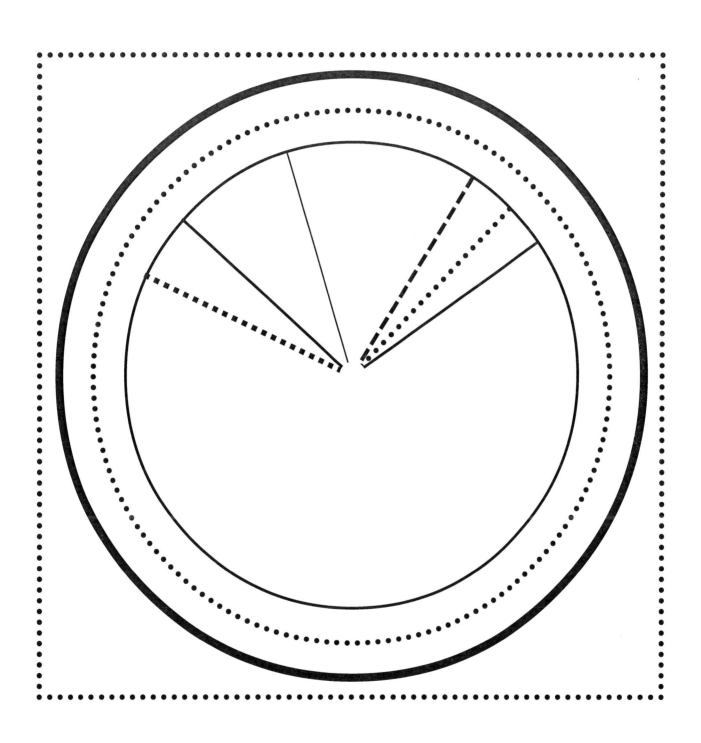

Comfort

Formula # 3: Clearing an Overwhelmed Mind

Use this formula when you are:
- ~ Exhausted
- ~ Overwhelmed
- ~ Confused
- ~ Out of balance.

Directions:

Find a quiet place if possible, where you won't be disturbed for about twenty minutes. Begin by reading the first message and then gazing gently at the circle or graph that goes with it for approximately two minutes. A longer or shorter time may be necessary. Let yourself breathe and relax as much as possible. Don't worry if the images move around or change in any way. That just means the graphs are working and that your mind and body are relaxing.

Some emotions might come up as well. That also means the graphs are working. Just give yourself permission to let go of anything that is causing you pain or suffering.

If someone is with you, talk to them about some of the feelings that you're having. It could help you to gain perspective on your situation. Having perspective allows you to make the best decisions about what will help you now.

After you've finished going through the entire formula, let yourself rest for a little while. You are doing very well with such a difficult circumstance. Be sure to take things one at a time.

1. Take a few moments and breathe deeply.
Pay special attention to those places in your body
where you are feeling pain.
Just let them relax.

Presence

2. Ask for peace to come into your heart and bring it healing.

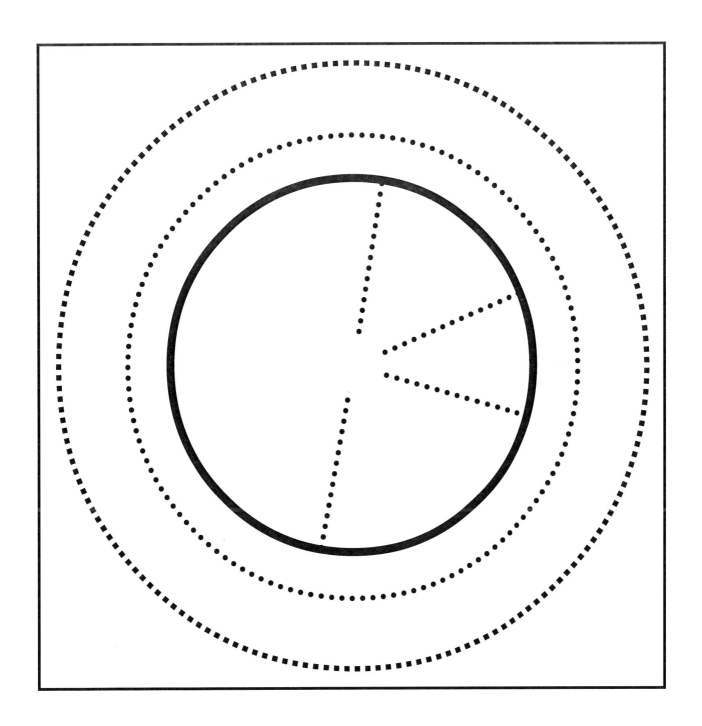

Receiving

3. You do not need to be perfect. Give yourself a break.

Balance

4. Focus your energy on taking good care of yourself now.
You are very important and what you do matters.
People care about you.

Compassion

5. You are being provided for.
Listen to your heart beating.
You are alive.

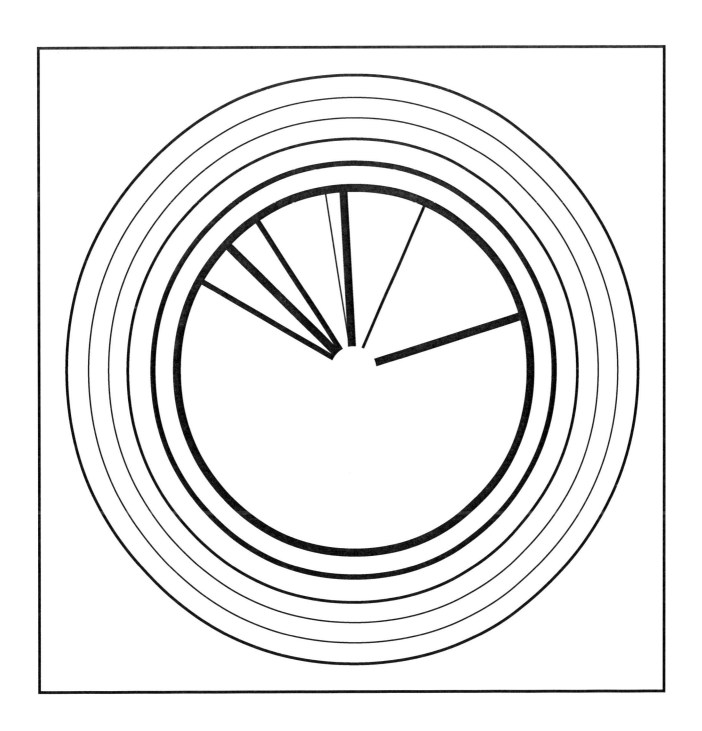

Nourishment

6. You are ready and able to make the changes necessary for you now.

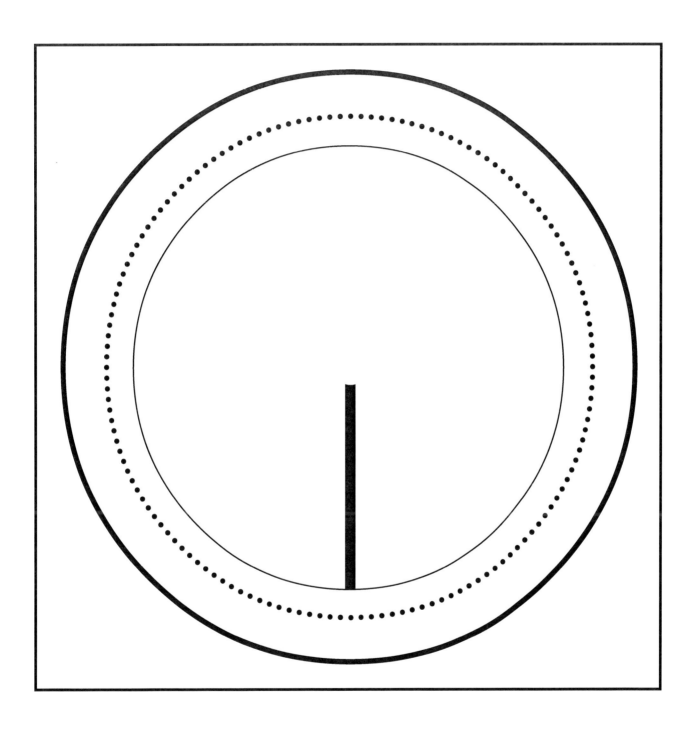

Change

7. Keep looking at the circle while you relax and think of something that you love very much.

Reunion

8. Notice how much better your body feels when your mind calms down.

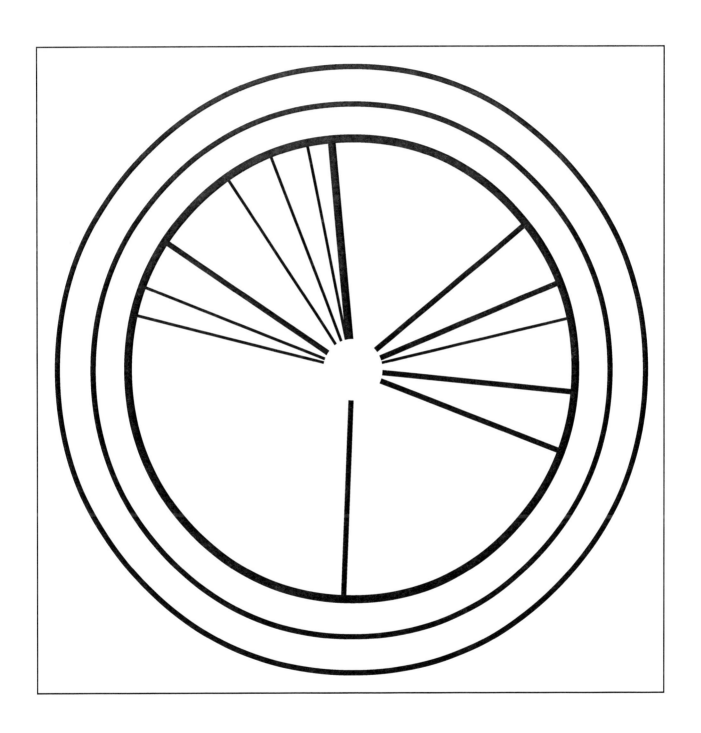

Integration

9. Take a deep breath and listen to that small, gentle voice that comes from your heart.
What is it telling you?

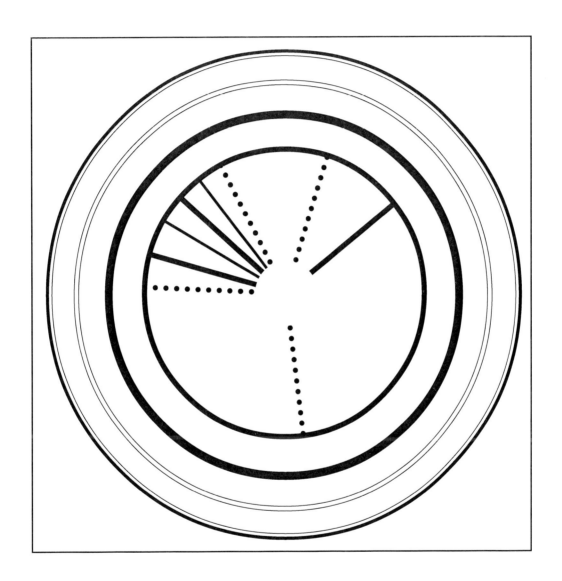

Inner Guidance

10. Let a calm feeling come from your heart and fill up your entire body - all the way to your fingertips.
Now it's time to rest.
Remember to take good care of yourself.

New Beginnings

Shock

Use this circle when you:
- ~ Are feeling stuck
- ~ Can't stop thinking about negative experiences or people
- ~ Are experiencing a flashback and want to break out of it
- ~ Cannot relax when you are experiencing spasms
- ~ In shock and cannot focus your mind
- ~ Feel trapped
- ~ Are experiencing inner conflict
- ~ Are caught in a fixed or compulsive state of mind.

Directions:

Take several deep breaths and relax while you are looking at this circle. Continue for several minutes until you feel yourself calming down.

If you want to enhance the action of the circle, imagine that you can use it to focus in on the thought, experience or conflict that is causing your problem, like a bull's eye.

You may get a conscious image or message, or you may not. Once you have a sense that your mind has found the target or fixation, imagine that you are sending a beam of light directly to the problem. Allow your lazer beam to break up the fixation and dissolve it until it is gone. Then you might check to see if there are other fixations or problems that you can do the same with.

Clear Your Inner Conflicts

Panic Attacks

Use this circle when you are:
- ~ Feeling uneasy or anxious
- ~ Having self-destructive thoughts
- ~ Living dangerously by taking reckless chances and being careless.

Caution: *the use of this circle is not intended to take the place of appropriate medical and/or psychiatric care. If you are having thoughts of suicide or extreme panic, seek help immediately.*

Directions:

To enhance the action of this circle, take several deep breaths and imagine yourself in an environment that is completely safe and peaceful. You are absolutely calm and protected here. Keep looking at the circle until you feel that the episode has passed.

Calm Your Mind

In Conclusion

The purpose of Soul Oriented Solutions has been to give you additional resources to turn to when you are going through difficult times. You are encouraged to share this information with others whom you feel might benefit from it.

Consider it a gift from someone that has been there and wants to share the little wisdom she has gained from her own experiences. Each formula has the potential to give some hope, inner guidance and clarity of mind if you are willing to try something new and different.

The Intuitive Learning Circles and Graphs used in this booklet have been specifically selected from several larger collections available through Soul Resources. If you would like to know more about them; contact information is listed below.

Finally, we want to hear from you about your stories of hope and inspiration. The mind is a powerful instrument. It can be your best friend or your worst enemy. If Soul Oriented Solutions has helped you to strengthen your belief in yourself, even in the smallest way, it has achieved its aim.

To ask questions, request a training or share your experiences, visit either of our websites at:
www.SoulResources.net
or
www.IntuitiveLearningCircle.com

Soul Resources
11201 Haines Avenue NE
Albuquerque, New Mexico 87112
(505) 271-4612